Panther Chameleon

The Ultimate Panther Chameleon Pet Owner's Manual

Panther Chameleon breeding, where to buy, types, care, temperament, cost, health, handling, diet, and much more included!

By: Lolly Brown

Copyrights and Trademarks

All rights reserved. No part of this book may be reproduced or transformed in any form or by any means, graphic, electronic, or mechanical, including photocopying, recording, taping, or by any information storage retrieval system, without the written permission of the author.

This publication is Copyright ©2019 NRB Publishing, an imprint. Nevada. All products, graphics, publications, software and services mentioned and recommended in this publication are protected by trademarks. In such instance, all trademarks & copyright belong to the respective owners. For information consult www.NRBpublishing.com

Disclaimer and Legal Notice

This product is not legal, medical, or accounting advice and should not be interpreted in that manner. You need to do your own due-diligence to determine if the content of this product is right for you. While every attempt has been made to verify the information shared in this publication, neither the author, neither publisher, nor the affiliates assume any responsibility for errors, omissions or contrary interpretation of the subject matter herein. Any perceived slights to any specific person(s) or organization(s) are purely unintentional.

We have no control over the nature, content and availability of the web sites listed in this book. The inclusion of any web site links does not necessarily imply a recommendation or endorse the views expressed within them. We take no responsibility for, and will not be liable for, the websites being temporarily unavailable or being removed from the internet.

The accuracy and completeness of information provided herein and opinions stated herein are not guaranteed or warranted to produce any particular results, and the advice and strategies, contained herein may not be suitable for every individual. Neither the author nor the publisher shall be liable for any loss incurred as a consequence of the use and application, directly or indirectly, of any information presented in this work. This publication is designed to provide information in regard to the subject matter covered.

Neither the author nor the publisher assume any responsibility for any errors or omissions, nor do they represent or warrant that the ideas, information, actions, plans, suggestions contained in this book is in all cases accurate. It is the reader's responsibility to find advice before putting anything written in this book into practice. The information in this book is not intended to serve as legal, medical, or accounting advice.

Foreword

Are you living an uneventful life and want to add a little something to brighten it up? It is time to have a pet—but not just any ordinary pet. While dogs and cats are lovely, they are not an option if you want to spice up your life. You should find a pet that is fascinating, can be easily tamed and exotic: the Panther Chameleon!

Having a pet will bring many benefits to your life—companionship, affection, loyalty, and love. Your life will be enriched as you will learn so much and you will feel happier. Emotionally, it has been proven that having pets decreases anxiety, stress or depression. Often, just looking at your pet and spending time with it will bring a satisfaction and joy without you knowing it. Animals have their own unique beauty, especially exotic ones like the Panther Chameleon.

Table of Contents

Introduction 1

Chapter One: All About the Panther Chameleon 3

    Panther Chameleon in Focus.. 4

    The Panther Chameleon's Excellent Vision 7

    The Panther Chameleon's Remarkable Feet 9

    The Panther Chameleon's Powerful Tongue 10

    Panther Chameleon's Distinctive Feature: Color Shifting 11

    A Panther Chameleon's Basic Diet 14

    Behavior and Temperament 14

    Courtship and Reproduction 15

    Enemies in the Wild... 16

    Conservation Status... 17

Chapter Two: The Panther Chameleon Care Sheet............... 19

    Housing 20

    Temperature... 21

    Lighting 22

    Humidity 23

    Cleaning the Enclosure... 23

    Diet and Eating Habits 25

        Food 25

        Vitamin and Supplements 27

Water 28

Sit and Wait Predator 28

Sleeping Behavior 29

Common Health Problems 30

No to Co-Habitation 31

Chapter Three: Choosing and Bringing Home Your First Panther Chameleon 33

Are you ready? 34

Choose a reputable breeder 39

Check for signs of a healthy Panther Chameleon. 39

Preparing the New Home 42

Feeding Tips 47

Chapter Four: Common Illnesses of Panther Chameleons and How to Prevent Them 53

Stress 54

Edema 56

Parasites 57

Metabolic Bone Disease 58

Upper Respiratory Infections 60

Calcium Deficiency 61

Vitamin A Deficiency 62

Egg Binding 64

Dehydration 65

Gout 67

Mouth Rot 68

Bodily Injuries 69

Tongue Problems 71

Shedding 72

When to Take Your Panther Chameleon to the Vet 73

What To Do When Your Panther Chameleon is Hissing . 75

Never Rescue a Chameleon from the Wild or A Poorly One 77

Chapter Five: Handling a Panther Chameleon Properly 79

Chapter Six: The Panther Chameleon as a Pet 87

Chapter Seven: Life Cycle, Reproduction, and Frequently Asked Questions 99

Mating and Breeding in Captivity 100

Panther Chameleon Hatchling Care 103

Reproduction in the Wild 104

Common Mistakes Panther Chameleon Pet Owners Make 105

Frequently Asked Questions 111

Conclusion 118

Photo Credits 121

References 122

"Breeding Panther Chameleons" -
Pantherchameleonworld.com 124

Introduction

The etchings on the skin of the Panther Chameleon are very attractive and are bound to get your attention! Panther Chameleons have unique eyebrows, curved tail endings and the ability to move their eyes independently to 360-degrees rotations. They have powerful, fast tongues that give them excellent hunting prowess. Chameleons are famous for their outrageous length of their tongue — they measure more than one and a half of the length of its body! Panther Chameleons come in a wide range of colors specific only to them. Add the fact that they can shift their body

Introduction

color rapidly through the movement of their pigment cells — what else could be more amazing than owning a Panther Chameleon for a pet!

While the idea of having a Panther Chameleon may excite you at the onset, you should also heed this word of caution: they are not for newbies or casual pet owners. If it's your first time to have a reptile pet, read on to find out tips on choosing your first Panther Chameleon, learn about its eating, sleeping and mating habits, and other care sheet information. You will also come across proper handling techniques that will help you have the best time with your Panther Chameleon. There are so many amazing facts about Panther Chameleons that you can discover in this book.

Owning and maintaining chameleons as pets can prove to be a daunting task and you have to be truly serious about this endeavor. But if you are up for a thrilling ride, then consider bringing this unique and appealing creature into your home. A pet chameleon is not for everyone — so why not be counted as one of the few who with the privilege of calling a Panther Chameleon your own? It can be the best choice you will ever make!

Chapter One: All About the Panther Chameleon

Chameleons, scientific name *Chamaeleonidae*, are interesting reptiles. They are a very unique and distinguished lizard species. They have a lifespan of two to eight years, depending on their living conditions, and usually live a solitary lifestyle. Chameleons are distinct because they have large eyes and coiled tails. Their body is covered in scales and they come in many colors: brown, black, green, tan, yellow and red—although they can shift colors, and that is what makes them very fascinating and distinctive.

Chapter One: All About the Panther Chameleon

Chameleons can be seen throughout different deserts, tropical forests and jungles in Asia, Africa, and some locations in North America and Southern Europe. It is believed that there are more than a hundred and eighty diverse species of chameleons. Some are a couple of feet long while others are just a little more than an inch (from 2.8 centimeters to 68.5 centimeters). The smallest and largest chameleon species are native to Madagascar. The smallest chameleon, pygmy leaf, measures less than three centimeters in length. The largest chameleon species, the Malagasy giant, grows to about 70 centimeters long. Another large chameleon species also found in Madagascar is the Parson's chameleon, which can develop to about 60 centimeters long. Chameleons' weight ranges from .01 kilograms to 2 kilograms.

Panther Chameleon in Focus

A Panther Chameleon (*Furcifer pardalis*) is called as such because of its spotted markings that make it appear like a panther and its forked feet. The name *Furcifer pardalis* is from the Latin *furci* which means "forked" and *pardalis*

Chapter One: All About the Panther Chameleon

which means "spotted like a leopard or panther". It is one of the more colorful species of chameleons.

Over the last couple of decades, the Panther Chameleon has become more popular because of the stunning and impressive array of colors and its curious behavior. Hobbyists, pet owners, and breeders prefer the Panther Chameleons imported from Madagascar. In the beginning, the Panther Chameleon had the reputation of being a difficult reptile to care for because imported chameleons came with poor conditions and health issues such as infections, dehydration, wounds, parasites, poor immune system and depression. In the early 1980s, importing these exotic animals was difficult and captive propagation programs as well as care protocols were set in place to improve the survival of Panther Chameleons. The efforts to improve husbandry and care were successful and today, there is a growing number of more robust Panther Chameleons in the market.

More and more people choose captive-bred Panther Chameleons compared to wild-caught ones for a variety of reasons: the age of a Panther Chameleon caught from the

Chapter One: All About the Panther Chameleon

wild cannot be ascertained and the health or lifespan cannot be determined for sure. However, advanced breeders or hobbyists love to care for and acclimate imported Panther Chameleons.

The brilliant color phases of the Panther Chameleon will tell you, from which part of Madagascar they come from, such as the cities of Nosy Be, Ambanja, Sambava, Ambilobe, Tamtave, etc. Male Panther Chameleons are larger than females, ranging from 15 to 20 inches long. Full-sized, mature female Panther Chameleons grow up to 8 or 10 inches in length.

You can easily tell the gender of Panther Chameleons—the males' skins are spiky and horny while the females' skins are usually smoother. Male Panther Chameleons are aggressive and they protect their territories, hence the horns.

Panther Chameleons in the wild, their natural habitat, usually have a short lifespan. They can live for about one or two years, largely because of the perils of disease, parasite infection and predators. Male Panther Chameleons bred in captivity usually live up to 4 or 6 years, or even up to 8 or 9

Chapter One: All About the Panther Chameleon

years in excellent conditions. Captivity decreases a female's lifespan. Female Panther Chameleons in captivity has a lifespan of 2 to 3 years after laying eggs. Virgin females, because they are free from the burden of reproduction, can live up to 8 years in captivity. When they are well taken care of, Panther Chameleons are robust and healthy and can live their whole life cycle.

The Panther Chameleon's Excellent Vision

Panther Chameleons, like all species of chameleons, are known to have excellent eyesight. They can see up to 10 meters from where they are. They are capable of moving their eyes in a 360-degrees fashion so they can see all around their body. This specialty allows them to spot their prey as well as catch sight of predators. Panther Chameleons also have the special skill of seeing ultraviolet light. In contrast, the Panther Chameleon's hearing is rather poor and can only function within a limited range.

What's so special about a chameleon's eyes? Other than the fact that they can rotate their eyes in a 360-degree fashion, they are the only animals that have the ability to

Chapter One: All About the Panther Chameleon

transition between their monocular and binocular vision. They can see things with each eye independently. The chameleon's eyes, located on the opposite sides of its head, can rotate with total freedom and provide a view in front, behind and of the sides.

How does this special ability help chameleons survive in the wild? While they are in search of prey, they utilize their monocular vision on each eye. The eye movements on both eyes are uncoupled—there are two separate bundles of eye nerves that function, allowing the Panther Chameleon to have a panoramic view of its surroundings with both eyes providing two separate images to the brain. . When the chameleon catches sight of its prey, both the eyes are coupled and they lock on the object. Once the eye movements are in sync, there is one image only and the head rotates towards it. The chameleon then uses its tongue to catch its prey. The same happens when there is a predator around, and the chameleon responds with a defensive action.

If you want to understand this amazing ability of the Panther Chameleon to switch spontaneously from

Chapter One: All About the Panther Chameleon

uncoupled to synchronous eye movement, think of as watching two movies in your head at the same time and when you want to focus on only one movie, you can do so without restrictions.

The Panther Chameleon's Remarkable Feet

Since they usually live on trees, the Panther Chameleons' feet are just right for clinging to tree surfaces. They have clustered or *zygodactylous* toes, razor-sharp claws and pads on their foot that allow them to grip branches and vines like pincers. Compared to other lizards, chameleons clutch their legs underneath their bodies to help them stay balanced and give them a rather athletic posture. Panther Chameleons, like most, use their long, curvy, muscular tails to get a good grip, especially when they use their tongues to catch prey.

Chapter One: All About the Panther Chameleon

The Panther Chameleon's Powerful Tongue

Panther Chameleons have very, very long tongues. Most species have tongues that are lengthier than their bodies. A Panther Chameleon can shoot out its tongue with the speed of 26 body-lengths per second. You won't be able to follow it with your unaided eye as it is the equivalent of more than 21 kilometers per hour! This mind-numbing speed of extending their sticky tongues is helpful in catching fast-moving insects that are part of a chameleon's diet. A Panther Chameleon can catch a prey that is at a distance of more than one and a half of its body's length.

Studies have shown that "catapults" are responsible for a chameleon's ability to propel its tongues at lightning-fast speed—the tongue increases speed from zero to twenty feet per second. The Panther Chameleon's tongue can go from zero to sixty meters a second. This flick of the tongue happens in a span of 20 milliseconds, so fast that you cannot see it. Scientists have found that there is a biological spring in the chameleon's tongue that allows such extreme movement. The catapult—elastic collagen tissues that are

Chapter One: All About the Panther Chameleon

flanked by the accelerator muscle and the tongue bone of a chameleon—stores then releases energy when triggered, propelling the tongue tip in the same manner a bow releases an arrow.

Panther Chameleon's Distinctive Feature: Color Shifting

When you hear the word *chameleon*, you immediately think of an animal that can change its colors. This is one of the reasons why chameleons are highly preferred exotic pets. Panther Chameleons can change their skin's colors to blend with their surroundings and protect themselves from predators or attack their prey. These colors—such as brown, black, yellow, blue, orange, tan, pink, red, green, turquoise and light blue allow chameleons to disguise themselves.

Recent studies have shown that when Panther Chameleons change their colors, it indicates a change in their emotional levels. They also change colors when their body temperature adjusts to the temperature of their surroundings or when they are communicating with other chameleons or their human owners.

Chapter One: All About the Panther Chameleon

Two popular myths about chameleon changing their colors are (1) chameleons camouflage or change their colors to harmonize with their environment and (2) All chameleons can change their colors. Truth is, chameleons don't just change colors so that they can match their habitat. The change happens as a response to the temperature and light around them, as well as their moods and way of communicating to others. The Panther Chameleon, for example, transforms to yellow and red colors when they are furious and when they are getting ready to strike. This advises humans and other chameleons to withdraw.

Of course, they do change their colors to hide from predators and to sneak up on their prey. But often, male Panther Chameleons will shift into bright colors when they want to attract females who are nearby.

Chameleons that can change into yellow, blue, red, turquoise, purple, black, brown, green or orange often shift to darker shades when the temperature is cold then lie out in the sun to warm up. To cool themselves when it is hot, they shift to lighter colors as these reflect the sun more effectively. Studies have also revealed that when Panther Chameleons

Chapter One: All About the Panther Chameleon

are in a good mood, they show off brighter colors, and their colors become darker when they are stressed.

Not all chameleons have the ability to change their colors, only some species do—and among those who could, some species can change into many colors while others are limited to changing to only brown, gray or green.

Chameleons that can shift from one color to another can do so because of chromatophores. A chameleon's outer skin layer is transparent and these chromatophores are unique cells that are clustered under said layer. The upper layer of skin of the Panther Chameleon contains red and yellow pigments, while the lower layers consist of melanin and a colorless, limpid substance. These chromatophores modify the visible red and yellow pigments on the skin's outer layer, creating myriad of colors. The melanin influences the intensity of the final color on the outer skin layer. Panther Chameleons, and other chameleons that have the ability to change colors, can shift from one color to another in a span of twenty to thirty seconds.

Chapter One: All About the Panther Chameleon

You can easily discern how your Panther Chameleon is feeling or what it is about to do simply by observing its coloration.

A Panther Chameleon's Basic Diet

The Panther Chameleon is an omnivorous animal. Some chameleons are vegetarians, others prefer a carnivorous diet. The Panther Chameleon will eat leaves, berries, fruits, worms, snails, and insects. Large chameleons often stalk and eat smaller reptiles. Learn more about a Panther Chameleon's diet and eating behaviors in the Care Sheet.

Behavior and Temperament

Panther Chameleons are territorial reptiles. If you are thinking of getting multiple panthers as pets, you should provide individual housing. If you make the mistake of housing two males together, they can attack each other. They

Chapter One: All About the Panther Chameleon

also do not like to be handled too much and they get stressed with a lot of fussing over. You can learn more on how to handle a Panther Chameleon in a dedicated chapter of this book.

Courtship and Reproduction

A Panther Chameleon's ability to shift colors is a skill that is not achieved until it is sexually mature, which comes when they are 5 to 9 months old. Male Panther Chameleons come in a wider variety of colors than females. Their colors are more vibrant when they are expressing their moods or communicating. A male that is fired up, defensive, aggressive or courting can display exciting and vivid shades. On the other hand, females have less color varieties and the dramatic ridge on the side of the head is smaller and less prominent. Likewise, the female hues come in softer hues of rose, peach or violet when they are receptive or amorous to the courtship of a male. If they are ill-disposed or gravid, they will show off extremely contrasting color such as black mixed with bright pink, red or orange.

Chapter One: All About the Panther Chameleon

A female Panther Chameleon can lay up to an average of 20 eggs. When the female is ready to lays her eggs, she digs a 10 to 30 - centimeter hole in a hole on the ground and buries them there. It takes from four to 12 months for a chameleon egg to hatch, depending on the species.

Enemies in the Wild

Most chameleons are small in size and animals like birds, mammals and snakes often feast on them. Panther Chameleons rely greatly on their ability to camouflage to avoid predators. They lay completely still and shift colors to blend in with their surroundings. In case a predator is unavoidable and camouflage won't help them escape, Panther Chameleons won't try to run away. Like most chameleons, they are slow moving reptiles. Instead, they will project themselves as a bigger reptile, be aggressive and hiss in order to scare off the attacker.

Chapter One: All About the Panther Chameleon

Conservation Status

Chameleons are threatened with environmental problems such as deforestation and pollution. Some species are already endangered and at risk of extinction. In the international pet trade, the Panther Chameleons is one of the most wanted chameleon species. This is because of the beautiful coloration of this species and the success of captive breeding. However, its population in the natural habitat remains stable. What is facing danger is its habitat because of environmental changes.

As was said in the beginning of this book, the Panther Chameleon can be quite a handful and it is not advisable for newbie reptile pet owners. However, it is not an impossible task and if you are up to the challenge, you can find more information about Panther Chameleons in the Care Sheet chapter of this book.

Chapter One: All About the Panther Chameleon

Chapter Two: The Panther Chameleon Care Sheet

So you've decide to get a Panther Chameleon for a pet…you are in for an exciting journey! While these reptiles may not live very long in captivity, you will enjoy their passive demeanor and weighed against caring for other lizards, having a Panther Chameleon is fairly easy.

Deciding to bring a Panther Chameleon home is a huge decision. Before you get to the part of choosing and buying one, you need to do a careful research about this species then check whether caring for one can fit your budget and schedule. Following are some of the

Chapter Two: The Panther Chameleon Care Sheet

requirements in caring for a Panther Chameleon such as housing, temperature, lighting, humidity, food, etc. It is important to learn all that you can about how to care for a Panther Chameleon before you make the step of getting one so that you can make the necessary physical preparations as well as get your heart, mind and pocket ready for the responsibility.

Housing

Panther Chameleons thrive in a ventilated enclosure. You should not put a chameleon in a glass terrarium, fiberglass mesh or metal mesh because they need proper air circulation and enough space. A mesh enclosure made of PVC coated hardware cloth is good.

You should also provide a vertical space for your pet Panther Chameleon to climb on as they prefer to be off the ground most of the time. The size of your enclosure should be able to accommodate long, sturdy branches and non-toxic plants. A good dimension for a cage is 36 inches long, 36 inches wide and 36 to 48 inches tall. You can provide an

Chapter Two: The Panther Chameleon Care Sheet

outdoor cage for your pet when the weather is warm, but be careful not to expose the chameleon to too much heat.

Panther Chameleons love to climb and you can use branches of ficus trees in their homes. Make sure that your branches are perched securely. You can include hibiscus, dracaena, pothos and vines. Do not put rubber plants and umbrella plants. Wash the plants thoroughly before including them in the cage to wash away any pesticide. A good foliage will allow your Panther Chameleon to feel safe in its enclosure as it is close to its natural habitat. Additionally, real plants will help raise humidity levels in mesh enclosures.

Temperature

The temperature of the enclosure during daytime should be between 75 to 90 degrees Fahrenheit. The basking spot should be at a minimum temperature of 95 degrees Fahrenheit. During nighttime, the lowest temperature of the enclosure should never drop below 15 degrees Fahrenheit.

Chapter Two: The Panther Chameleon Care Sheet

- To provide heating, place an incandescent or basking light in a ceramic heat component or a reflector. Make sure to put these outside of your enclosure to avert any danger of burns.

- Place the branches a different heights where there will be different temperatures, so that the Panther Chameleon can go to them depending on how they are feeling, like for sleeping and basking.

Lighting

Invest in a good ultraviolet bulb for a light source in your enclosure. Panther Chameleons need UV light turned on for about half of the day, 10-12 hours at least. The Zoomed Reptisun 5.0 is a good UVA/UVB bulb. When the outdoor temperatures are suitable, you can let your Panther Chameleons bask in natural sunlight—just make certain that there is an available shad that the chameleon can go to when it feels too warm.

Chapter Two: The Panther Chameleon Care Sheet

Humidity

You should have a 60 to 85 percent humidity level in your enclosure as Panther Chameleons require above average humidity. Get a hood hygrometer so you can measure and maintain go humidity levels.

Misting your living plants regularly will keep the enclosure fresh and if you can invest in a misting or drip system, it is the best option. A drip system should be placed in such a way that water droplets will flow over the plants. You will notice that unlike other pets, chameleons will hardly drink from a water bowl. You will see them lapping up water droplets from plants. This is the reason you should get a good drip or mist system—it is also your pet's water source.

Cleaning the Enclosure

A clean home is a good home. Your cage should be kept hygienic so that you can avoid the onset of mold and bacterial growth. Line the cage with newspaper or paper towels so that it will be easy for you to clean the cage. You

Chapter Two: The Panther Chameleon Care Sheet

can put your plants in pots so there will be live vegetation with less cleaning. Avoid substrates like wood chips as they can be accidentally ingested and could cause your pet to become sick.

Make sure to remove any dead things such as dead bugs, mold, fecal matter or shed skin in your enclosure so that parasites or bacteria will not grow.

When cleaning the enclosure, remove your chameleon so that it won't be bothered. For the cleaning solution, you can put a bit of dishwashing soap in water in a spray bottle. Spray on floors and walls and on plastic plants if you have them. Then clean it off with a paper towel. Mist your enclosure then dry off with another paper towel. Make sure that you don't get soapy water on the real plants. It is important to clean your enclosure every day or every two days

Chapter Two: The Panther Chameleon Care Sheet

Diet and Eating Habits

Food

- While Panther Chameleons will also eat some plants, fruits and vegetables, they are mainly insectivores. You should provide your pet a variety of insects such as flies, silkworms, grasshoppers, roaches, locusts and especially crickets which are their favorites. You can feed them waxworms, mealworms and superworms, too. Give them these worms as variety, but not too much as they are quite fatty.

- Get your insects from the pet store. Catching insects from the wild is dangerous as these insects may have been exposed to pesticides. Don't worry crickets and other insects are inexpensive. Also, never ever give fireflies, bees or wasps to your Panther Chameleon.

- To make sure that your Panther Chameleon is getting enough nutrients, you should gut load your insects with fresh veggies and vitamins before you feed them to your pet. Dust them with Vitamin D3 and calcium supplements twice a week, and a comprehensive vitamin-mineral supplement weekly.

- Make plant matter available such as sugar snap pea pods, mustard greens, turnip greens, kale, romaine lettuce, dandelion greens and collard greens. Chop the veggies into bite-sized pieces.

- If you notice that your Panther Chameleon is gaining too much weight and there are uneaten insects in the enclosure, you should cut back on feeding amounts and frequency. There will be periods when your Panther Chameleon will eat very little or none at all. This comes as a result of seasons and weather. If the chameleon looks and acts normal and healthy, there is no cause for worry. Provide it with food even if he doesn't eat it. Take note that it is wise never to leave live prey in the Panther Chameleon's cage because there is the possibility that the insects can attack your chameleon.

Chapter Two: The Panther Chameleon Care Sheet

- Mice can also be part of your Panther Chameleon's diet. You should give pinkie mice—these are newborn mice and they don't have any fur. They provide nutrients and vitamins. But since they are high in fat, you should only give pinkie mice once or twice a month as a treat. To be more humane when it comes to feeding, use pre-killed pinkie mice. You can buy them frozen from pet stores and they are inexpensive. Completely thaw them in warm water before giving it to your Panther Chameleon.

Vitamin and Supplements

Get Vitamin D3, calcium and other multivitamins in powder form from your local reptile pet store. You can apply multivitamins to your pet's food as advised. Light dusting is enough; you don't have to pour a lot of supplement powder on your chameleon's food. Keep in mind that too much of a good thing is not good.

Chapter Two: The Panther Chameleon Care Sheet

Water

You don't have to put a bowl of water for your Panther Chameleon. As noted earlier, chameleons drink drops of water off leaves that come from the misting system. You can also use a dripper as a water supply. A dripper is a water vessel that has a tube and valve which slowly trickles water onto leaves. If you prefer handing water to your Panther Chameleon, you can use a spray bottle and manually spray fresh water onto leaves and other stuff in your enclosure where the pet can drink the water droplets from.

Sit and Wait Predator

Chameleons often hide in trees and bushes while waiting for their prey. They use their zygodactylous toes and prehensile tails to stay on branches while they hunt, eat, and rest. They don't stalk their prey; they just patiently wait until the potential meal comes close enough for them to catch using their tongues. Their natural green or brown skin color

Chapter Two: The Panther Chameleon Care Sheet

naturally blends with branches and leaves so they are camouflaged—they don't necessarily change their colors to hide from their prey before attacking. They remain deathly still while using their 360 - degree view to track insects and other prey. When they focus on one prey, they use both eyes to measure distance then strike with their super-fast tongue. Their prey wouldn't even know what hit them.

Sleeping Behavior

Since Panther Chameleons are experts at perching on small branches, vines or twigs, the can sleep while clinging. Chameleons aren't rowdy animals and they will likely rest near the same place where they have stayed throughout the day. Others, though, will hike higher or go lower before it's time to sleep. The average perching height ranges from 1 to 3 feet off the ground.

Your Panther Chameleons will find clusters of leaves and stay there to sleep in order to protect itself from cold temperatures and predators. If by chance your pet chameleon has escaped its enclosure, you will most likey

Chapter Two: The Panther Chameleon Care Sheet

find it sleeping in small trees or shrubs. When Panther Chameleons sleep they sometimes display vivid colors. Often, they will drop at the slightest touch and fall on the ground. Scientists believe that this is part of their defense mechanism against attacks from nocturnal predators such as the nocturnal lemur, boomslang, and other nocturnal birds.

Common Health Problems

Panther Chameleons are prone to the following health problems:

- Stomatitis or mouth rot
- Calcium deficiency
- Vitamin A deficiency
- Metabolic bone disease

Stomatitis is an infection in a chameleon's mouth where there is excessive drooling and redness. Poor diet often results in deficiencies in calcium and vitamin A. But possibly the most serious and potentially fatal illness in a chameleon

Chapter Two: The Panther Chameleon Care Sheet

is the metabolic bone disease. Signs that your Panther Chameleon is suffering from metabolic bone disease include lethargy and loss of appetite. This is become its bones are becoming brittle and weak.

When you notice that your pet chameleon is showing signs of any of these ailments, consult a veterinarian that specializes in reptile care.

No to Co-Habitation

When you find success with one chameleon, you may think that it is okay to add another one in your enclosure. While nothing will prevent you from getting more than one chameleon in your care, you cannot put them in one cage. You cannot even put the cages beside each other as this can cause undue stress and agitation which leads to serious health issues. Panther Chameleons of the same gender do not cohabitate well in shared cages.

Chapter Two: The Panther Chameleon Care Sheet

Panther Chameleons are not social animals and will only interact for reproductive purposes or when they are protecting their partner and their territory. Chameleons don't have to exhibit signs of stress or aggression for you to realize that they cannot live near each other. Male Panther Chameleons don't have to be in the same cage to be aggressive to another male chameleon. Even reflections on glass enclosures can cause them to feel belligerent. They can send each other subtle signs of hostility until one of them—or both!—become so stressed that they get sick.

The case is different for breeders as they can put hatchling and juveniles together in small groups with enough water, food, and basking and perching space as well as visual barriers. When the young Panther Chameleons reach about 3 months of age, they should be separated in individual enclosures.

Chapter Three: Choosing and Bringing Home Your First Panther Chameleon

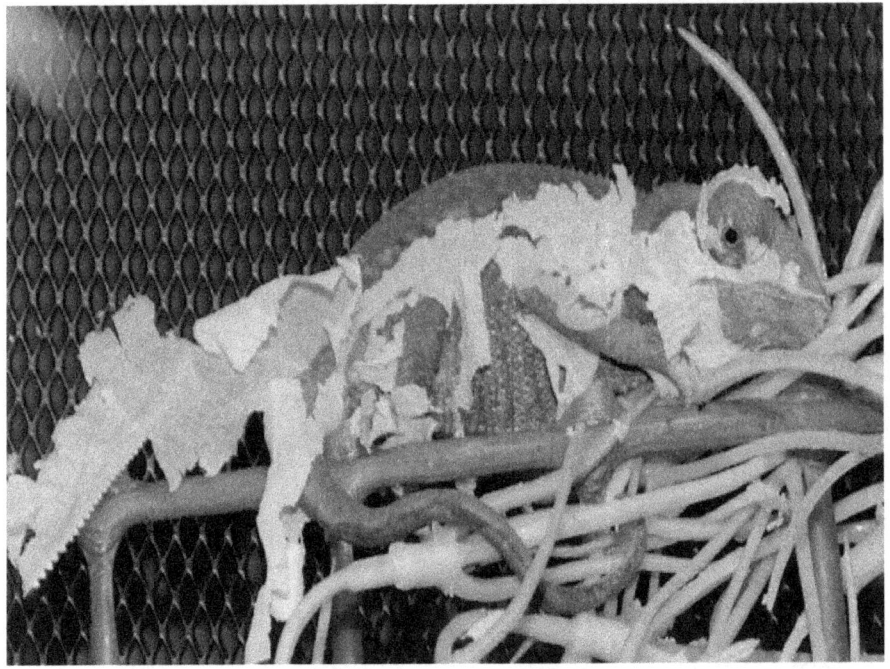

Now that you've learned about the needs and behaviors of a Panther Chameleon, the search begins! Since this will be your first chameleon pet, you need to pick the right one for you. There are many factors to consider.

Chapter Three: Choosing and Bringing Home Your Panther Chameleon

Are you ready?

First of all, are you ready to not just buy but care for your first chameleon? You need to check you budget and see if you are ready to make that commitment. As a rough estimate, you will spend the about $900 to 1500 for one year of care (this includes supplies, food and vet care, on top of the cost to purchase a baby chameleon. Not only does it cost money, but also energy and time in cleaning and monitoring the Panther Chameleon's enclosure on a daily basis. To help determine what is involved in the care of a chameleon, talk to people who already own one as well as reptile experts.

Wild - caught vs. captive - bred Panther Chameleon?

You should refrain from getting wild-caught chameleons for pets. Here are a number of reasons:

- Chameleons that have been captured from the wild are transported to and traded in different countries then sold to a reptile enthusiast, breeder or hobbyist. Wild-caught chameleons are usually stressed or

Chapter Three: Choosing and Bringing Home Your Panther Chameleon

depressed from the long transport and they have poor health.

- Wild –caught chameleons are usually infected with parasites from their natural habitat.

- You cannot determine the age of wild-caught Panther Chameleons; you may be getting one that is on its last year of life.

- The captive-bred species are readily available in the market.

- Captive-bred Panther chameleons grow up in very good, safe conditions and are healthy when they are sold.

- You can check the parents of captive-bred Panther Chameleons and easily identify its age.

Chapter Three: Choosing and Bringing Home Your Panther Chameleon

- You can get a fecal sample and have a veterinarian examine it for parasites so you can be sure that you are getting a healthy one.

- A captive-bred Panther Chameleon is already used to living in enclosures so you won't have a hard time making it adjust to its new home.

- The price of captive - bred Panther Chameleons is lower than those caught from the wild.

Decide which kind of Panther Chameleon you like.

There are many questions you need to answer first before you purchase your first chameleon.

- Do you want a male or a female Panther?
- What type/locale do you like?
- What kind of colors are you interested in?
- Do you want a Panther with coloration or you are willing to wait until it matures?

Chapter Three: Choosing and Bringing Home Your Panther Chameleon

- Are you getting a baby Panther Chameleon or one that is a little bit mature?

- If you decide on a baby, do you have access to small insects that are good to feed baby chameleons?

- Male panthers have bright and intense colors but females are also very pretty, although mostly pink in coloration. Once you have made up your mind on the gender of your Panther Chameleon pet, you should start browsing through the different locales. The top favorites are the Ambanja, Ambilobe and Nosy Be because of their beautiful colors.

- The age of the baby Panther Chameleon should be considered carefully. If it is your first chameleon, it is not advisable to get a young one below 3 months old. The first three months of its life are the most fragile. Once Panther Chameleons get past the 3-month mark, they are healthier and stronger. As a first time pet owner, you may not have the ability or capacity to

Chapter Three: Choosing and Bringing Home Your Panther Chameleon

provide the best care for very young panthers, even if you have the best of intentions. Moreover, 3 month old baby Panther Chameleons will not show their colors yet so you may want to wait until they are a bit mature, especially if there is a coloration that you prefer. It is a good idea to get an older baby Panther Chameleon so that you can see the developing colors and get a picture of how it will look like as it grows older at home with you.

- Once you have decided on the gender, locale and age, it is time to see babies from different breeders. Keep in mind that breeders will have a variety of baby panthers at different times of the year. It is generally unsafe to transport baby Panther Chameleons during winter so you should get one during spring, summer or fall.

Chapter Three: Choosing and Bringing Home Your Panther Chameleon

Choose a reputable breeder

To ensure that you are purchasing a healthy Panther Chameleon, you should buy from a trustworthy pet store or breeder. Don't just buy from the first chameleon breeder you encounter. Get recommendations from a veterinarian for exotic animals. If your local pet store does not sell chameleons, they may be able to give you recommendations of where to buy. You can also check out reptile magazines and reptile shows for more information.

Check for signs of a healthy Panther Chameleon.

Once you've found a breeder or pet store, you should look for a healthy chameleon to purchase. Even if you feel bad for a poorly cared for Panther Chameleon, you should never bring home a sickly one, especially if this is your first time to care for one as a pet. To spot a healthy Panther Chameleon, you need to be on the lookout for the following:

Chapter Three: Choosing and Bringing Home Your Panther Chameleon

- **Clear, bright and alert eyes.** When the chameleon's eyes are sunken, it could be dehydrated. Likewise, if the chameleon eyes are always closed, it could be sick.

- **Straight limbs.** Chameleons with bowed or bent legs may have metabolic bone illness.

- **Strong grip on branches.** A Panther Chameleon with a flexible casqued is not healthy.

- **Clear, vivid coloration.** While brown is a normal color on a chameleon's skin, a dark shaded or crab-looking chameleon could be too cold or suffering from an illness.

- **Clean mouth.** When there are chees-like or green patches on the chameleon's mouth, it could be suffering from mouth rot.

Chapter Three: Choosing and Bringing Home Your Panther Chameleon

- **Clear skin.** The chameleons should not have any scratches, wounds or bruises. Dry skins or patches in the skin are signs of parasite infection.

- **Alert disposition.** Lethargic chameleons that have difficulty breathing and a lack of appetite may have a respiratory infection. Consequently, a chameleon which keeps making crackling noises when it is breathing, or keeps gaping its mouth, may also be suffering from a respiratory infection.

Make sure that you choose an active and alert Panther Chameleon. Chameleons are not keen on being held so if you are holding one and it is not resisting you by hissing or gaping its mouth, then it could be sick. Upon request, the breeder or the pet store staff can perform a routine fecal exam to determine if the chameleon has parasites and needs deworming. If you are choosing from a set of juveniles, you need to avoid the ones that are smaller than their siblings, because they may not be feeding well and growing

Chapter Three: Choosing and Bringing Home Your Panther Chameleon

slowly. Moreover, be sure to check the enclosures where the chameleons are kept. It is a sign of how they are being cared for.

- **Do not buy Panther Chameleons online.** It is best to have a good look at the baby panther before you make a purchase so you can check if it is healthy or sick and injured. Additionally, chameleons fare poorly when they are shipped and the panther that you bought online could be stressed while being shipped, get sick or even die.

Preparing the New Home

Before you even make the purchase, you need to have prepared the Panther Chameleon's new home first. You should start planning and preparing your pet's home even before you deiced to get one. You already know the basic requirements for Panther Chameleon care from the previous

Chapter Three: Choosing and Bringing Home Your Panther Chameleon

chapter. Here are some simple tips to get your new pet's enclosure ready for the time it will come home:

Choose a good cage type and size for your new pet.

Keep in mind that Panther Chameleons grow quickly so you should get a big enclosure. Don't get a small one in the beginning then get a bigger one when your pet grows. It will only cost you double. The minimum size requirement for chameleon enclosures is 36x36x48 inches.

If you live in a warm place, you can use a wire cage, a tall bird cage or a screened cage. You can also use a glass terrarium or a vivarium as it has insulation materials that can protect your pet. You can get a cage from your local pet store.

The enclosure should be placed in a quiet area.

Chameleons don't like noise and too much movement. By keeping them away from distractions and loud sounds,

Chapter Three: Choosing and Bringing Home Your Panther Chameleon

they will be less stressed. Make sure that the home of your Panther Chameleon has plenty of shade and will not in the path of continuous direct sunlight where you will place its cage to avoid overheating.

Add substrates.

Substrates are materials you will use to line the bottom of your chameleon cage. When deciding on which substrate to use, keep in mind that it should be comfortable for your Panther Chameleon and, at the same time, easy for you to clean.

Good substrates are paper towels, butcher paper and newspaper. Bad substrates include sand, wood chips and moss. These materials may be accidentally swallowed by your pet and it can cause internal blockage, as well as ingestion of mites, mold and bacteria.

Make sure that you clean the bottom of the enclosure using bleach and water and replace the substrates once a week.

Chapter Three: Choosing and Bringing Home Your Panther Chameleon

Add foliage and branches to your Panther Chameleon's new home.

Even if they are bred in captivity, it is inherent for Panther Chameleons to want a natural, arboreal environment. Plenty of non-toxic plants as well as branches will give the desired effect. Choose and place branches in a manner that will allow the Panther Chameleon to use his feet—various diameters and orientations as well as horizontal and vertical placements. Secure the branches so that your pet won't get hurt.

Choose the right kind of foliage. You can add fig trees, philodendrons and bamboo palms. In Panther Chameleon Care Sheet it is mentioned that hibiscus, ficus and pothos plants are the most popular choices. Mist them daily as they are also the chameleon's water source.

Provide good lighting.

UV light bulbs will not only provide light but also heat that your Panther Chameleon needs. You may also need

Chapter Three: Choosing and Bringing Home Your Panther Chameleon

a basking bulb that provides a temperature of 90 to 105 degrees Fahrenheit. Next to the basking bulb provide a fluorescent bulb that will emit UVB/UVA light that your Panther Chameleon needs to activate vitamin D3 in its body.

Secure your lights so they don't fall on your pet chameleon. Do not use heated rocks in the basking area or as a heat source—your pet could be burned. You don't need night lights. While the nighttime temperature should not fall below 15 degrees Fahrenheit, the temperature should not be too warm. A room thermometer can help you monitor the temperature in your chameleon's enclosure. Make sure to switch bulbs once or twice a year.

Now that your Panther Chameleon's home is ready, you can go make that purchase for the baby panther!

Chapter Three: Choosing and Bringing Home Your Panther Chameleon

Feeding Tips

Now that the Panther Chameleon is home, your journey of caring for it will start. Here are some feeding tips that can help you as you take care of your new pet:

Measure out crickets for your Panther Chameleon.

How much and how often your Panther Chameleon will eat depends on a number of factors: species, gender, size and age. Measure out the proper size and number of crickets to feed your pet. The general rule is that you should not feed your chameleon with a cricket that is bigger than its head width. If you have a baby aged three months old, you should give it as much crickets as it can eat. Put in some fruit flies and small, sliced fruit. Panther Chameleons that are between 3 - 6 months old can eat as much as 10 - 12 crickets daily. Chameleons aged 6 - 12 months can have 10 - 12 crickets every other day. Adults should only eat 7 - 10 crickets every other day.

Chapter Three: Choosing and Bringing Home Your Panther Chameleon

Feed your Panther Chameleon in the morning.

Set a time in the morning to feed your pet chameleon. When they feed in the morning, they digest their food better.

It is important to set a schedule that you can work out with your daily routines. Keep in mind that you have to gut load your insect feeders a few hours before you can give them to your pet chameleon. You should be consistent with this schedule so that your chameleon will remember feeding times. Routines are especially helpful when it comes to preparing your chameleon for handling. You can keep track of feeding schedules using a calendar or planner. To avoid overfeeding or skipping mealtimes, make sure you check the dates off in your planner once your pet is fed.

Provide the Panther Chameleon's food free-range.

Chameleons are hunters. So put a few insects in the branches or leaves that are relatively near your pet chameleon. You can also put them on rocks and other items

Chapter Three: Choosing and Bringing Home Your Panther Chameleon

on your enclosure like furniture. Don't forget to close the enclosure after you put the insects in.

Watch to see if the chameleon spotted the insects. Once they do, they will move slowly towards their prey. If the chameleon does not move towards its prey, it may have not seen it or it could be sick. That's why it is important to see if your Panther Chameleon has noticed the insects and starts to feed on them.

Don't leave live crickets all at once in the cage, and take out uneaten live insects. They may be hiding under rocks, leaves or other objects so make sure to inspect. These crickets can be aggressive and hurt your pet at night.

Provide water supply by misting.

Chameleons do not drink from a water dish or bowl but off plants.

Chapter Three: Choosing and Bringing Home Your Panther Chameleon

Provide leafy greens and fruits.

Your Panther Chameleon may enjoy an occasional leafy green in its diet. Make sure to spray the leaves lightly with water and check if your pet will eat them. You can also put fruits like mango, apple or orange. If your Panther Chameleon won't eat the leafy greens and fruits, do not worry. It may be that your pet is more of an insectivore than an omnivore. Remove uneaten veggies and fruits so that they won't cause mold and bacteria to grow in the enclosure.

Did you know that you can also feed your Panther Chameleon in a cup? You can use any kind of plastic cup as long as it is tall enough (at least 8 oz.) to keep insects from bolting out.

Use an opaque and not a transparent cup. If the insects are in a transparent cup, the Panther Chameleon may not realize that there is a cup and injure itself while trying to get the insects out using its tongue.

Place the cup quite near the chameleon so he can spot the insects. The chameleon will most likely come from above

Chapter Three: Choosing and Bringing Home Your Panther Chameleon

the cup so place it low on the enclosure. You can punch holes in the plastic cup and hang it from a pant inside the enclosure.

Again, be sure to measure out the appropriate amount of insects that matches your chameleon's age and dietary needs. If you are regularly feeding your Panther Chameleon from a cup, it will get used to it and learn that food appears in the cup. When it is hungry or it is time to eat, you will notice that your Panther Chameleon may be hanging out near the feeding cup. Use the same feeding cup for your chameleon. If you have more than one, take care not to mix the cups to avoid spreading germs among them.

Chapter Three: Choosing and Bringing Home Your Panther Chameleon

Chapter Four: Common Illnesses of Panther Chameleons and How to Prevent Them

Panther Chameleons thrive with proper care. All animals are prone to diseases and it is no different with your Panther Chameleon. Read on and find out about common illnesses that ail most reptiles so that you can watch out for symptoms and warning signs from your pet. This chapter aims to educate you, help you prepare and prevent your Panther Chameleon from contracting any illness. A word of caution: never, ever play vet. Always seek professional help

Chapter Four: Common Illness of Panther Chameleons

for treatment. Just because you know about something, it doesn't mean that you can provide medical treatment.

Stress

A Panther Chameleon can be stressed because of poor lighting, too much lighting, loud noises, too much traffic, too much handling, too much movement, being squirted with cold water, and drastic changes to its habitat. It can be stressed by seeing another chameleon, seeing another animal, and even seeing its own reflection. You can identify if your Panther Chameleon is stressed by checking for the following signs:

- Watery feces
- Smelly feces
- Vividly dark color change
- Dramatic changes in color
- Different body temperature
- Loss of appetite
- Constantly rocking its body

Chapter Four: Common Illness of Panther Chameleons

- Flattening its body
- Abnormally aggressive
- Excessive hiding in the plants

Stress will take a toll on your pet's health, bring a host of illnesses and shorten its lifespan. You can prevent your Panther Chameleon from being stressed by taking the following measures:

- Do not handle your pet too much or do not handle it at all. Depending on its personality, you should look out for signs of your Panther Chameleon's receptivity or tolerance to handling and respect its desires.

- Keep your Panther Chameleon away from your other pets. It's been said again and again in this book that you cannot put two chameleons close to each other. Chameleons are also wary of other animals near them and can feel afraid, uncomfortable or threatened. They are so anti-social that they don't even want to see their on reflection. Glass enclosures are

Chapter Four: Common Illness of Panther Chameleons

discouraged as well as other materials that may reflect their image back to them. If you are taking care of a wild-caught chameleon, you should provide a very natural environment so that it won't be stressed with the drastic change.

Edema

Edema is the inflammation of the body brought about by excess fluids in the hypodermal layer of the skin. This swelling may be caused by excess vitamins, usually dusted on crickets and feeders. When the Panther Chameleon's enclosure is too humid, swelling can also happen.

Take a close look at your Panther Chameleon and check for swellings that appear like goiter in its neck, throat and chest. To prevent your pet from developing edema, make sure to do the following:

- Avoid gut-loading your Panther Chameleon's food with too much vitamins and mineral supplements.

Chapter Four: Common Illness of Panther Chameleons

- Do not give your Panther Chameleon to much protein-laden food.
- Make sure that the humidity is at right levels all the time.
- Bring your Panther Chameleon out of its enclosure to bask in natural sunlight. Often, pets develop edema by staying too long in their enclosures.

Parasites

Lack of proper hygiene can cause parasitic infection. Likewise, feeding your Panther Chameleon with insects caught from the wild may cause them to be infected with parasites such as protozoa, trematodes, cryptosporidium and nematodes.

To check for the presence of parasites in your Panther Chameleon, the veterinarian should check your pet's fresh dropping. To collect a sample, use a glass or plastic container. The dropping is composed of brown excrement and whitish urine element. Once you caught the dropping, put it in a baggie so it won't be desiccated. Then keep it in the refrigerator until you can take it to the vet. You won't be

Chapter Four: Common Illness of Panther Chameleons

able to see parasites with your naked eye that is why you need a veterinarian to check it.

Treating parasitic infection is very difficult and can be stressful to both you and your pet. To prevent your Panther Chameleon from contracting parasitic infection, you should:

- Maintain a hygienic enclosure. Clean it every day.
- Check the feeders that you give your pet to make sure they do not contain parasites.
- Never feed your Panther Chameleon with insects that you caught, even if it is just from your garden.
- Purchase insects from your local pet store or via online.

Metabolic Bone Disease

Panther Chameleons need sufficient supply of UVB light for at 10 – 12 hours a day in order to process the calcium that they get from their food. The best source of UVB is natural sunlight, but if it is not available, you can use

Chapter Four: Common Illness of Panther Chameleons

UVB bulbs. If Panther Chameleons don't get enough UVB light, they can develop metabolic bone disease which can lead to growth defects and premature death. Metabolic bone disease is a slow process. Be sure to check your pet for signs of this disease such as:

- Clumsiness
- Bowed legs
- Rubbery jaw
- Trouble climbing
- Loss of appetite
- Tongue issues

To prevent your Panther Chameleon from contracting this disease, it is important to ensure that it gets enough sunlight. A periodical check should be made to detect negative symptoms. Early detection is important and if you see the signs present, then bring your pet to the veterinarian immediately.

Chapter Four: Common Illness of Panther Chameleons

Upper Respiratory Infections

Environmental contamination, husbandry issues and poor caring often cause upper respiratory infections in Panther Chameleons. When the chameleon has an infection in the lungs, it has pneumonia. To identify if your pet chameleon is suffering from respiratory infections, check for the following signs:

- Wheezing sounds
- Gaped mouth
- Excessive mucus
- Popping sounds
- Bubbling around the nose
- Mouth rot and bubbling
- Inflammation

Respiratory problems can aggravate your Panther Chameleon and increase its stress levels. To avoid such situations, be sure to:

- Check the quality of air in the enclosure often to make sure it is properly ventilated

Chapter Four: Common Illness of Panther Chameleons

- Always maintain proper temperature
- Always take out the litter from the bottom of the cage
- Make sure the water source is always clean
- Check the insect cultures of your feeders
- Always maintain a clean enclosure

Calcium Deficiency

Calcium is stored in the ones but is used in the body to flex muscles. However, when there is lack of calcium in the muscles, the Panther Chameleon will get it from the deposits in its bones resulting in weaker bones. When your Panther Chameleon intakes too much phosphorous and insufficient amounts of Vitamin A, it can result in calcium deficiency. Of course, inadequate amounts of calcium are also a factor. All these vitamins and minerals should be provided to make sure your pet is healthy. Symptoms of calcium deficiency include:

- Lethargy

Chapter Four: Common Illness of Panther Chameleons

- Lack of appetite
- Soft bones
- Soft jaw
- Physical deformities

To prevent calcium deficiency in your Panther Chameleon, you should:

- Dust your feeders with calcium
- Gut your feeders with healthy fruits and greens

Vitamin A Deficiency

In the wilderness, Panther Chameleons have no lack of Vitamin A as it is abundant in nature. However, in captivity, their diet of insects may lack vitamin A and this poor nutrition can lead to a deficiency. Signs of lack of vitamin A include the following:

- Loss of appetite
- Stunted growth
- Swollen eyes

Chapter Four: Common Illness of Panther Chameleons

- Swollen limbs
- Abnormalities in the skin
- Abnormalities in the bones
- Hemipenile
- Liver enlargement
- Upper respiratory infections

Your pet Panther Chameleon should get proper nutrition if you want to avoid this deficiency. Make sure to:

- Coat your feeder insects with multi-vitamin supplements rich in vitamin A at least twice a month.

- Occasionally feed your Panther Chameleon with apples, oranges, sweet potatoes, cornmeal, carrots, legumes, mustard seeds and rolled oats. These are rich in vitamin A.

Chapter Four: Common Illness of Panther Chameleons

Egg Binding

Reptiles have the common problem of retaining their eggs. This condition happens when the female Panther Chameleon cannot reproduce mature eggs, causing anatomical defects, dehydration and malformed eggs. The female will also be in poor condition, have the wrong temperature and will not make a good nesting site.

Even though they are have big, swollen abdomens, pregnant chameleons are always active—eating, drinking and moving around. To know if your Panther Chameleon is suffering from egg binding, you should check if:

- The pregnant Panther Chameleon becomes lethargic, inactive or depressed
- The pregnant chameleon raises her hind limbs (as if giving birth) and yet no eggs are produced

You need to be watchful and get your pet chameleon to the vet immediately because egg binding, when untreated, can lead to death. To best way to prevent your

Chapter Four: Common Illness of Panther Chameleons

female Panther Chameleon from suffering from this condition, is to ensure that:

- She gets adequate nutrition through proper diet and the needed supplements
- Provide a good substrate that will become her nesting site.

Dehydration

Dehydration is fatal to many pets and it is true of Panther Chameleons. It can be caused by insufficient water supply, having inadequate places in the enclosure to hold water, or because of other internal illnesses. You can check if your Panther Chameleon is dehydrated when you notice the following symptoms:

- Loss of appetite
- Sunken eyes
- Yellow or orange urate
- Weak skin (skin that does not go back to normal when you pull it)

Chapter Four: Common Illness of Panther Chameleons

To avoid dehydration and potential death, you should:

- Provide adequate foliage in the enclosure where the Panther Chameleon can drink from

- If your Panther Chameleon is not drinking from drops of water off leaves and vines—which is should naturally do—consider putting a small bowl of water in its home.

- Make sure that the misting or dripping system is working properly so that there is enough hydration available.

- If your husbandry, watering and misting are all good and the Panther Chameleon is still not drinking and dehydrated, you should bring your pet to the vet. There may be an underlying cause for its condition. Remember early detection can save your pet's life.

Chapter Four: Common Illness of Panther Chameleons

Gout

Just as gout is caused by uric acid in people and other animals, the same is true for reptiles. Gout is a serious condition for Panther Chameleons; it comes in many forms and symptoms and should be immediately treated by a veterinarian.

There are primary and secondary gouts and you can detect if your Panther Chameleon is suffering from it when it exhibits the following symptoms:

- Swelling joints
- Reduced mobility
- Exhibiting pain when moving such as climbing or walking
- Showing extremely aggressive behavior when touched at the joints

A Panther Chameleon is a low-protein reptile and to keep it from developing gouts, you should:

- Avoid giving it food that contains a lot of proteins.

Chapter Four: Common Illness of Panther Chameleons

- Gut feed your insect feeders with only vegetables and fruits so they don't overload in protein
- Offer your pet chameleon a high-variety diet and not just insects.

Mouth Rot

A chameleon may suffer from mouth rot due to the following causes:

- Overcrowding
- Improper phosphorous
- Wrong temperature regulation
- Insufficient calcium and other vitamins
- Poor nutrition
- Poor animal husbandry
- Bodily injury such as scratch

You will know that the Panther Chameleon has an oral problem when:

Chapter Four: Common Illness of Panther Chameleons

- Yellowish brown stains are visible around the teeth and gums
- There is slight swelling of the lower jaw
- There is visible dehydrated matter surrounding the mouth

Mouth rot should be treated quickly, otherwise the Panther Chameleon will lose its appetite and its health will deteriorate. To prevent this condition:

- Provide proper nutrition
- Ensure that the Panther Chameleon does not eat anything that can injure its mouth
- Keep the enclosure closed to avoid foreign animals or object from entering in.

Bodily Injuries

No matter how much you protect your Panther Chameleon, it is bound to have minor bodily injuries in the form of scrapes, scratches and cuts through the course of regular movement and play. However, some bodily injuries

Chapter Four: Common Illness of Panther Chameleons

can be serious especially when it results from accidents such as being hit when the enclosure is knocked over or when a bulb falls. Whether the injury is minor or major, you should ascertain that your Panther Chameleon is being treated and you should watch over it carefully while it recovers.

Some injuries can be easily seen while some may be hidden and you have to watch your pet carefully to notice if it is in pain. Another way to identify an injury is to regularly check the Panther Chameleon's body for cuts, scratches or scrapes on its skin. You need to do this because when you notice injuries, you can treat them immediately and prevent infections. To prevent incidents of bodily injury:

- Ensure that your Panther Chameleon is healthy by feeding and treating it right. When the Panther Chameleon's body is healthy and strong, it won't get injured easily.

- Take extra care when handling your pet chameleon, especially if you are getting it from a branch or a tree.

Chapter Four: Common Illness of Panther Chameleons

- Place your enclosure in a safe place, away from large pets that may accidentally knock it over.

When a Panther Chameleon has large lesions or is sporting a limp, you have to bring it to the vet to prevent septic infection.

Tongue Problems

Tongue issues can result from vitamin deficiency, muscular problems in the mouth or a mouth infection. When injured, the main organ that the Panther Chameleon uses to eat won't be pulled back into its mouth. When this happens, you have to make sure that the tongue does not dry up. Check for symptoms of tongue issues:

- Swollen gular area
- Swelling of the tongue
- Cannot remove the tongue while feeding
- Cannot use tongue
- Failure to feed

Chapter Four: Common Illness of Panther Chameleons

When this happens, make sure that your Panther Chameleon gets medical attention. To prevent the condition,

- Give your Panther Chameleon proper nutrition
- Gut load insect feeders with vitamins and calcium
- Provide adequate UVB light
- Provide adequate water in the dripping/misting system

Shedding

While it can be normal for reptiles to shed a bit of skin, excessive shedding in Panther Chameleons means that there is something wrong. You may also notice flaky pieces of skin in the bottom of its enclosure or on the branches it usually perches on.

To prevent shedding, make sure that your misting system if working properly — or you can mist our pet lightly to help in the painless removal of its skin. If your Panther

Chapter Four: Common Illness of Panther Chameleons

Chameleon is constantly shedding, you need to check for underlying causes such as vitamin deficiency, dehydration or an illness.

When to Take Your Panther Chameleon to the Vet

Taking care of a Panther Chameleon is not easy and you will often find yourself facing different situations. Chameleons have evolved from living in the wild and they are very adept at hiding any illness while they are in captivity.

You may be afraid of bringing your Panther Chameleon to the vet for fear that handling can cause them unnecessary stress, but here are some symptoms you should not ignore. You won't easily notice them and your pet could be suffering from an illness for a long time before you do, so when you observe these visible symptoms, you should immediately take your pet to the vet:

- Injuries in the arms, legs, head or body
- Sunken eyes

Chapter Four: Common Illness of Panther Chameleons

- Difficulty walking
- Coughing or crackling sound
- Respiratory infections
- Limited movement
- Difficulty climbing
- Sore mouth
- Excess mucus
- Abnormally dark shades (a sign of stress)
- Loss of appetite
- Sleeping for long periods of time

Like any other pet, exotic animals like Panther Chameleons are susceptible to infections. Get them to the veterinarian immediately so that the illness doesn't prove fatal. This doesn't mean that you have to be paranoid and look at your chameleon the whole time, just be attentive for warning symptoms and do not delay when you need to take action. If you are a responsible owner, your chameleon will live its full lifespan.

Chapter Four: Common Illness of Panther Chameleons

What To Do When Your Panther Chameleon is Hissing

When your pet chameleon is hissing, it is experiencing stress either from handling or temperature. Make sure to back away from your pet chameleon when it is hissing and ensure that its surrounding environment is at the right temperature. Chameleons hiss when they are frightened or they want to ward off contact. Do not attempt to touch or handle your Panther Chameleon when it is hissing.

It is also good to look around for reasons that may causing your Panther Chameleon to hiss, especially if you have another chameleon near its enclosure—it may be exhibiting an aggressive behavior towards it.

Make sure you provide a safe environment for your Panther Chameleon so it doesn't feel scared, aggravated or uncomfortable. It will thrive well in a peaceful and calm environment. Follow the advice on the care sheet regarding the size, contents and other requirements for a chameleon's cage so that your pet will enjoy being in captivity.

Chapter Four: Common Illness of Panther Chameleons

Chameleons can also hiss when they are in pain. Your pet can suffer from metabolic bone disease if it isn't exposed to sunlight. They manufacture vitamin D3 through absorbing natural sunlight. When they lack vitamin D3, they can become crippled. Supply them with artificial heat and light if natural ones are unavailable.

To avoid hissing and aggressive behavior in the future, you should limit handling your Panther Chameleon. When agitated, your chameleon may even bite you. Even though it is not harmful or toxic, it can be quite painful. Additionally, too much handling can bring chronic low-level stress to your pet and it will have poor health. Chameleons, like people and other pets, have different temperaments. Some like to be handled, others shun touch. Always observe your Panther Chameleon closely so that you know if it likes your touch. If so, you can tame it. If not, be content to watch it inside its enclosure.

Another important thing is to watch out for illnesses or injuries. Panther Chameleons hiss when they are suffering discomfort. Other than metabolic bone disease, your chameleon can suffer from injuries in their bodies, legs or

Chapter Four: Common Illness of Panther Chameleons

feet. They may also get eye infection. Pain can cause them to act out against you. If there is a suspected injury or illness, contact a veterinarian immediately for a checkup. If your Panther Chameleon is sick or injured, you may need to put it in a smaller, clean cage to help it heal.

Never Rescue a Chameleon from the Wild or A Poorly One

It has been said in the beginning of this book that in choosing a pet Panther Chameleon, you should only buy a captive-bred one. Not only are wild-caught chameleons stressed, they also carry a lot of parasites from the wilderness. There is no reason to get a chameleon from the wild because natural populations are fast depleting. It is better to purchase form breeders in captivity so you can get healthier ones and not add to the threat to the continuity of chameleon species.

It is in this note also that you should remember never to rescue a chameleon from the wild. Again, it can be highly

Chapter Four: Common Illness of Panther Chameleons

stressed and loaded with parasites. You can get sick. Also, you should resist the temptation to save a chameleon that you see is poorly cared for—for the same reason. Not only should you think about the health of the chameleon that you will get for a pet, you should foremost think of your own health and safety. Make sure the Panther Chameleon is healthy and safe before you bring one home.

Chapter Five: Handling a Panther Chameleon Properly

Having a Panther Chameleon for a pet is not like having a dog or cat that you can cuddle. Unlike other reptiles like geckos or pythons that can tolerate being touched or carried, chameleons don't take a liking to handling and can be easily stressed. A lot of people treat chameleons the same way they do fish—watch and don't touch. However, this doesn't mean that you cannot handle your Panther Chameleon anymore. Like turtles, you need to learn the proper manner and frequency of handling them.

Chapter Five: Handling a Panther Chameleon Properly

Panther Chameleons have their own personalities and may have different responses to handling. Some are docile, some are aggressive, some are easily terrified and some are friendly. It is also good to know that with some time and careful handling sessions, Panther Chameleons that are previously opposed to handling may turn around for the better.

As a Panther Chameleon pet owner, you should know that handling goes beyond simple holding. You may experience a hissing and biting pet and it is not as fun when it is time to administer medication or to bring it to the vet for a checkup. Nevertheless, you need to know how to properly handle your pet especially if you need to care for it and take it out of life-threatening situations.

Here are some tips on how to best handle your Panther Chameleon:

Give your pet chameleon some time to settle in its new home.

Like any pet of any age, it will take some time for an animal to get used to its new home and its new owner before

Chapter Five: Handling a Panther Chameleon Properly

it gets cuddly and inviting or even just slightly tolerant of handling. Panther chameleons are very sensitive reptiles when it comes to environmental changes and being in a new home will cause them stress. You will notice that they won't even eat in the first few days in their new enclosure as they are still getting a feel of it and adjusting. To get them familiar with their new home and routine, you should not disturb them by handling them for about a couple of weeks. Just feed them, mist the plants and clean the cage in the routine that you want established. You may feel impatient about waiting, but if you jump right in and try to handle your pet, you will find it more difficult in the long run.

Try hand-feeding.

The best way to a man's heart is through his stomach—and the same is true with chameleons. Don't just drop the insects inside the enclosure! Associate your hand with food so your Panther Chameleon will be acquainted with it and associate it with good things. When it gets used to your hand and your closeness, it won't feel fear. After

Chapter Five: Handling a Panther Chameleon Properly

your Panther Chameleon has settled in nicely in its new home, you can try hand-feeding it before you even attempt to handle it.

Now, you don't have to use your hand in the beginning. You can use a tong or tweezers to hold the insects, bring it at a close distance to your pet and wait for it to stick out its tongue and get the food. To get best results with hand-feeding, do it with the first feeder of the day. That way, your Panther Chameleon is most hungry and will most likely take it from your hand.

Do not put your hand or the feeder too close to your pet as they will feel nervous. Also, do not stare at your chameleon so as not o make it feel uncomfortable. Wait patiently until the insect peaks its interest, or hunger gets the better of it. Try hand-feeding just once a day. If you have been holding the food out for a few minutes and your pet chameleon does not strike at it, he is probably not interested so you should stop it for the day and do it again tomorrow. Response to hand-feeding may take days or eve weeks, but it is advisable to keep on trying until you succeed. Use tasty treats to entice your Panther Chameleon.

Chapter Five: Handling a Panther Chameleon Properly

Let them come out of their cage on their own.

Never, ever force them to come out of their cage, no matter how gently you do it. Your Panther Chameleon will feel so cornered in its cage and your huge hand is trying to grab it. It will try to run away, hiss or bite. Give it time to come out of its cage on its own terms, while you are in the same room. This will make your Panther Chameleon comfortable going out and exploring. Soon it will even try to climb up your hand, arm and shoulder.

What you can do is to leave door if its enclosure open and place a branch in front of it. Then sit in the vicinity so that your Panther Chameleon notices you are in the same room. It won't jump out as soon as you open the cage. It can even take hours, but eventually it will explore on its own. Try to do this every day and about the third time that it comes out, you will notice that it will do so as soon as you open the door. When it is comfortable going to the branch in front of its cage, you can place your hand in front of it, much like another trail it can walk on. Your Panther Chameleon

Chapter Five: Handling a Panther Chameleon Properly

will walk towards your open palm. Let him stay there a minute or two to enjoy your presence and be comfortable. When it isn't bothered, you can try to lift it up and allow it to walk over your hands then return him to the branch. This way, you will build trust and familiarity.

Do this every day and soon you will notice that your handling sessions will become longer as time goes by. Allow your Panther Chameleon to feel safe in your hands and you will not have any trouble handling it. As you have given it time to get out of its cage on its own and become used to it, it will also get used to climbing onto you and allowing you to carry it.

Handling should be associated with only good things.

In order to encourage your Panther Chameleon to get out of its cage, you need to associate the activity with good things such as basking in natural sunlight, playing with a plant, eating or roaming around. Chameleons love these activities and when they know that they can do these things

Chapter Five: Handling a Panther Chameleon Properly

when you open the door of their cage, you won't have a hard time getting them to go out.

Respect your chameleon.

Just because your Panther Chameleon now trusts you and is familiar with your handling, it does not mean that you should handle it all the time. Chameleons will react to different experiences differently depending on their mood. Some chameleons would easily be hand-fed but won't like climbing onto their owner's arm. They can be tolerant as long as you respect their space—much like humans would want you to respect their personal bubble. Other Panther Chameleons will love to climb on your hand or onto your shoulders but would never eat hand-fed food.

You need to learn to respect your Panther Chameleon. You will see signs of its discomfort, stress, or liking to the length of time it is out as well as the amount of handling it tolerates. As with any pet, use positive reinforcement and soon enough you will enjoy handling and spending time with your Panther Chameleon.

Chapter Five: Handling a Panther Chameleon Properly

Chapter Six: The Panther Chameleon as a Pet

As with owning any other pet, there are advantages and disadvantages. Here are some advantages of having a Panther Chameleon as a pet

Panther Chameleons do not require too much effort or direct interaction. Some high-energy pets can be so demanding. Fortunately for an owner who cannot handle such energy, Panther Chameleons are low-energy pets. Much like turtles, Panther Chameleons do not move too

Chapter Six: The Panther Chameleon as a Pet

much and won't require that you exercise with them or talk to them. If you are someone who is quite busy and you won't have time to take your pet for a walk or give it a cuddle every day, then the Panther Chameleon can be your best friend. Just make sure that it has an established daily routine of feeding time consisting of live food, regular and proper misting, branches to climb on and a clean and safe enclosure, then it will be happy. They don't require stimulation unlike other pets in order to stay happy.

While you may at some point enjoy a bit of handling, experts do not recommend handling beyond transportation when you need to clean its home or when you have to bring it for a checkup. Some of them may become too nervous and stressed with too much handling. But if you get to practice the handling techniques mentioned in a chapter in this book, congratulations! You can have some one-on-one time with your Panther Chameleon. Just keep the interaction to a bare minimum because no matter how sociable you think your pet is, it is naturally a solitary creature and will thrive best that way.

Chapter Six: The Panther Chameleon as a Pet

Panther Chameleons are beautiful!

You can take all day just looking at this uniquely interesting creature. Panther Chameleons are known to have vibrant colors plus the ability to change them. While this skill is useful to ward off predators in the wild, it is mostly just for show and communication when the Panther Chameleon is in captivity. Imagine having your own natural wonder at home!

You don't have to hire a pet sitter.

Whenever you want to go on a vacation, you don't have to pay a pet sitter to watch over your Panther Chameleon. In their enclosure, they will be able to drink or hydrate through an automatic misting system. While daily live feeding is a must, and you shouldn't leave live insects in the enclosure that can harm your pet, you can figure out a way for your Panther Chameleon to feed for those occasional times you can't spend the night at home.

Chapter Six: The Panther Chameleon as a Pet

Like most reptile pets, Panther Chameleons are hypoallergenic.

A lot of people have become allergic to dogs and cats that is why keeping reptiles as pets have become increasingly popular. A lot of people now keep fish, frogs, turtles, lizards and the likes.

You don't need a big space to keep Panther Chameleons.

Just follow the required size of the enclosure and you are good to go. Even if you live in a small apartment, a studio unit or a loft, you only need a terrarium—no need for running or walking area or a separate eating and sleeping place.

Panther Chameleons don't smell or make loud noises.

Panther Chameleons are never noisy like birds, cats and dogs. They also don't have the pungent smell of rodents. It takes less work to keep your chameleon home clean and odorless

Chapter Six: The Panther Chameleon as a Pet

You will find yourself being more interested and having the desire to learn more.

It will bring you such joy to possess a piece of Madagascar in your home. Herpetology, or the study of reptiles, is such an interesting and absorbing pastime. You will find yourself visiting reptile shows, checking our online forums and meeting other reptile-owners or breeders. While you may not have too much interaction with your pet, you can surely spend time and interact with people who have the same hobby as you.

It is easy to understand why people would want a captive-bred Panther Chameleon for a pet. But, again, taking care of one is not for the faint-hearted or the enthusiastic newbie reptile owner. Here are the disadvantages of owning a Panther Chameleon:

Panther Chameleons are difficult to maintain (but they are not the most difficult!)

Panther Chameleons need live food every day that should be given to them in a way that they can hunt for it. They don't

Chapter Six: The Panther Chameleon as a Pet

drink still water from water containers so you have to have a misting or dripping system in place. They also need live foliage in their enclosures and you need to clean it regularly.

A lot of things can stress a Panther Chameleon and this can lead to sicknesses.

- Panther chameleons, as with all species of chameleons, are NOT cuddly and they don't cuddle. If you are looking for a pet that you can snuggle with at the end of the day, or a pet that loves to be touched, the chameleon is not it.

- Panther Chameleons, like most reptiles, can be infected with parasites. The skin of reptiles can be home to different parasites and having a chameleon at home can bring the risk of parasitical infection, especially when you handle your Panther Chameleon or clean its enclosure. It is best to buy from a respected breeder instead of getting one from big pet

Chapter Six: The Panther Chameleon as a Pet

stores. And of course, do not bring home a chameleon caught from the wild.

- A Panther Chameleon is generally just a display animal. You can't expect your chameleon to be all happy and jumping into your lap when you arrive home. It will just perch there quietly in its chosen branch and you may often feel its indifference even if you are hand-feeding it. That is why you cannot treat it like your average household pet. Dogs and cats are quite sociable—birds and even pigs can be sociable too!—but chameleons are the exact opposite. Think of it as owning a fish or a snake. Be prepared for a life of silence with this pet.

- You can't put two chameleons together in one cage. Chameleons do not like sharing their homes and will fight and likely injure each other when placed together. You will have to settle for having a single Panther Chameleon or get more cages that require lots of space (because you cannot put the cages near

Chapter Six: The Panther Chameleon as a Pet

each other, as well) if you want to have more than one Panther Chameleon.

While having pets require dedication, time and attention, these things are a small price to pay for the joy that it brings. There are many mental, emotional and even physical benefits to getting a pet, exotic or otherwise. So if you are deciding to get Panther Chameleon for a pet, then you are on the right track because of the following reasons:

Pets will help reduce stress levels

In a fast-paced world, people become more and more stressed every day. While exercise, meditation and reading can help alleviate stress, one of the best ways is to have a pet at home. Enjoying the company of a pet can make you happy and reduce stress hormones. Especially with a Panther Chameleon, which is just quiet and often unmoving, you can sit back, relax and talk to it about your day, even pour your problems out. Pets are good listeners and the Panther Chameleon is the best listener of all. Even if you

Chapter Six: The Panther Chameleon as a Pet

don't want to talk, simply looking at its bright, beautiful colors will add joy to your life, especially after a hectic day. If you are feeling low, you don't have to sulk in your loneliness or stay in a negative place, get up and clean your pet's enclosure or feed it. If you feel like you aren't important, just think of how your pet needs you and how it depends on you. If your Panther Chameleon already trusts you and comes out of its cage willingly, you can have it rest on your shoulder so you can spend some quality time.

Pets are a constant companion.

There may be times when people won't be around whenever you need them and you cannot rely on social media connections—but your pet will always be there with you. Even if they are naturally quiet and not as expressive in their love and gratitude to you, as dogs or cats are, you know that your pet chameleon will be there for you. You can be yourself, be upset, be silly sing, cry, laugh, whatever—it won't judge you. Scientific studies have shown that constant loving companionship with animals is the one of the best

Chapter Six: The Panther Chameleon as a Pet

ways to improve health. This constant companionship helps improve your immune system, enhance mental health, boost heart health and even reduce physical pain. There are so many testimonies of the power of animal companionship, and a Panther Chameleon can provide just that.

Pets can provide you entertainment.

While other pets like dogs, cats, pigs, birds, and rodents can do tricks to entertain you, the Panther Chameleon won't lag behind. Its ability to change colors can be a source of entertainment that can keep you enthralled for hours. Depending on the personality of your chameleon, you can train it to climb certain obstacles. There was even a Panther Chameleon owner who trained his pet to wave! Being entertained engages your heart in laughter and joy, keeping boredom and sadness away.

Chapter Six: The Panther Chameleon as a Pet

Pets give you the opportunity to be responsible.

Whatever pet you choose to get, you will be the one to care for it. Stepping up to this responsibility will allow you to be more responsible in other areas of your life as well. While Panther Chameleons are not really suitable for first-time pet owners or young children, the daunting task of taking care of it will benefit many adults regarding consistent responsibility.

To sum it up, Panther Chameleons are really great pets to have. You don't have to rush into getting one, though. You need to carefully study all the care requirements of having one. Count the cost of not just the animal but also its housing, heating, food and water, lighting, veterinary visits and more. It is best to talk with friends who are already taking care of chameleons as well as professionals before you decide to bring one home.

Chapter Six: The Panther Chameleon as a Pet

Chapter Seven: Life Cycle, Reproduction, and Frequently Asked Questions

You don't have to know how to breed Panther Chameleons especially if it is your first chameleon pet, but learning about their mating behavior and how breeders raise hem in captivity is very interesting and will make you appreciate your pet even more.

Chapter Seven: Life Cycle, Reproduction, and FAQs

Mating and Breeding in Captivity

A Panther Chameleon will use its color-changing abilities to communicate to a chameleon of the opposite gender during breeding season. Both male and female sexually mature panther chameleons have this skill and will display specific breeding coloration to show that they are ready to mate. They also use visual signals as well as physical gestures. But to the casual observer, the carrying coloration is the most prominent sign that of chameleon courtship.

During breeding season, male Panther Chameleons will increase the intensity of their skin colors to attract females. They will also do a series of head nodding as a sign of courtship. If a female dislikes the male, she will show off a high - contrast coloration usually black or brown with bright pink, orange or red. If she likes the male, she will show off softer hues of peach, rose or violet. Once receptive, the Panther Chameleons will copulate and it can take hours or even days for the mating to be complete. Some breeders keep the male and female together for multiple mating

Chapter Seven: Life Cycle, Reproduction, and FAQs

sessions until such time that the female will reject the male. In other instances, the female is removed from the enclosure when the male becomes too aggressive.

Once mating is completed, the female becomes gravid or with egg, then the coloration in her stomach will change into a non-receptive one dark brown or black with high contrast colors. This will show that she has successfully mated and gestation will take 20 to 30 days.

While gravid, female Panther Chameleons can also change coloration in order to make threats to approaching males: they will gape their mouths open and rock back and forth. On the other hand, the successful male will either stay shortly with the female post-breeding or continue roaming around in search of another mate.

Around ten to fifteen days after successful mating, the female Panther Chameleon will stop eating until it is time for her to lay her eggs. When breeders see the female chameleon wandering around the bottom of its enclosure, they pick her up and place her in a laying bin. She needs to dig a tunnel so she can lay her eggs there. A laying bin is a

Chapter Seven: Life Cycle, Reproduction, and FAQs

10-inch deep container that is filled with moist soil. Breeders should not watch a female digging or laying her egg—this will stress her out and scare her and she will abandon laying her eggs. If she does this, she may die of egg retention. Breeders will know when the Panther Chameleon is done laying her eggs when she fills the hole she dug. The breeder should then take her out of the laying bin and put her back in her cage. The female should be provided with extra water and calcium-rich food and supplements.

Once the breeder removes the female, they dig up the eggs carefully from the tunnel that the mother made, and the eggs are kept in the same manner in which they are found. A clutch usually has 10 to 40 eggs but female Panther Chameleon lays an average of 20 eggs. The eggs are placed in a sealed container that has damp vermiculite. Two to three 1/16" holes are drilled into the container for ventilation. The container is stored in a dark and cool closet with temperatures of 65 to 80 degrees Fahrenheit and humidity levels of 80-90%, for 8-12 months.

Chapter Seven: Life Cycle, Reproduction, and FAQs

Panther Chameleon Hatchling Care

Caring for Panther Chameleon hatchlings are similar to how you care for adult panthers. There are just some slight differences. For instance, you can keep 15 hatchlings together—you can never do that with adult chameleons—in small enclosures that have the following dimensions: 15x15x20 inches. You can use plastic tubs or little screen cages. They are kept in the small containers until they are three to four months of age.

After that time, the hatchlings can be moved to individual cages with 16x16x20 inch dimensions. They can stay there until they are 9 or 10 months old, then moved to adult cages.

It is important to keep the hatchlings hydrated. They should be misted 3-4 times a day. They should also be fed frequently with fruit flies and tiny crickets.

Chapter Seven: Life Cycle, Reproduction, and FAQs

Reproduction in the Wild

The same courtship and reproduction happens in the wild. Breeding usually takes place between the months of January and May, but it varies depending on geographical locations. Some female Panther Chameleons can breed once a year, others multiple times. After mating and gestation, females will dig burrows using their front feet and back up into these burrows to lay about 10 to 40 eggs. After laying, they will bury their eggs and fill the tunnel with soil to hide their nest. Female Panther Chameleons often drag twigs and leaves over the nesting site to keep it from being discovered.

As you would have guessed, similarly with captive breeding, the mother no longer concerns herself with her young after she lays the eggs. The young are left to be independent starting at birth. After 6 to 12 months, the young chameleon will emerge from its egg by creating a star-shaped gap in one end of the eggshell using its egg tooth. The egg tooth is a hardened, sharp bulge on its upper jawbone that will eventually fall off as it grows. Hatchlings

Chapter Seven: Life Cycle, Reproduction, and FAQs

weigh from 0.25 to 0.75 grams. They will reach maturity after 6 months.

Both male and female Panther Chameleons will not display any parental involvement in their young other than creating eggs. The female's last maternal act is securing the protection of the buried eggs. However, the female, while gravid will take time and effort to ensure that her young fully develops within her during gestation. For instance, they will voluntarily expose themselves to UV light sources so that they have sufficient vitamin D in their body. The mother Panther Chameleon knows that without adequate vitamin D or proper diet, the embryos won't form their skeletons and there is a risk that the eggs will fail to hatch.

Common Mistakes Panther Chameleon Pet Owners Make

The Panther Chameleon is one of the most popular reptiles that people what to keep as their own. While you may have understood some of the work that it entails to

Chapter Seven: Life Cycle, Reproduction, and FAQs

bring a Panther Chameleon home, you also need to learn about the common mistakes that people make when they get chameleons for a pet. They underestimate the task of caring for this amazing creature and treat it as they would any ordinary pet. But with exotic pets, prevention is always better than intervention. Learn what not to do from the following list:

Mistake #1: The owner is not home enough.

While Panther Chameleons are not very sociable creatures and they do not require much social interaction, this doesn't mean that you can leave them alone at home for long periods of time. They can be affected by sudden changes in temperature and humidity and if you are not careful, even if you have installed an automated system, your pet can suffer. What will happen to your pet if the timer broke down or the misting malfunctions? You could go home to a dead pet. Similarly, Panther Chameleons prefer to hunt live food and there is the danger of putting too many

Chapter Seven: Life Cycle, Reproduction, and FAQs

insects/prey in their enclosures just because you will be out of the house for a long time.

If you really want to have a Panther Chameleon for a pet, then you should be prepared for the responsibility that comes with caring for it.

Mistake # 2: The owner practices careless handling of the Panther Chameleon.

Even with the handling techniques you learned in this book, you should always remember that chameleons are not really keen on handling and would be happier if they keep to themselves. Before you even touch your pet, be certain that you know the correct way of handling, your hands are clean, and that you won't cause undue stress. Content yourself with watching and observing until you learn the proper way of handling. If you want a pet that you can touch all the time, choose one that is not a chameleon.

Chapter Seven: Life Cycle, Reproduction, and FAQs

Mistake # 3: The owner does not realize when the Panther Chameleon is stressed.

You may think that just because chameleons walk slowly and you can easily grab them, they want to be touched. You can put them on your shoulder and they will stay perfectly still. This is not because they like it or they are content—they are not moving because they are stressed. Some chameleons will hiss and be aggressive enough to bite you when they feel threatened or scared, but most will just be too stressed and afraid to move. Do not mistake this for contentment on their part. It is not okay when your Panther Chameleon is not moving. It wants to be left all alone in its enclosure, on a branch or under a cluster of leaves. When you insist on holding it or carrying it simply because it is not giving an adverse reaction to you, then you are giving it a great deal of stress which can have negative effects on its health and even cause its lifespan to become shorter.

Chapter Seven: Life Cycle, Reproduction, and FAQs

Mistake # 4: The owner only gives the chameleon a simple diet.

Panther Chameleons, like all other chameleons, thrive on a high-variety diet. Just because crickets are a favorite doesn't mean you should give it every single day. Even if you dust your crickets with enough supplements, your Panther -Chameleon will still lack nutrients. They enjoy a variety of insects so don't limit them to two or three. Don't forget to add plants, as well. Ask your local reptile veterinarian about what you can best feed your Panther Chameleon so that it can enjoy a wide variety of food.

Mistake # 5: The owner provides a small enclosure or adds in another chameleon.

Yes, chameleons don't move too much but it doesn't mean you can put them in a small glass terrarium. It is in their nature to live in the wide wild world so they need a large habitat to live in even in captivity. You can't just put a couple of branches in a small aquarium and expect it to enjoy its home. It needs to have lush foliage, lots of branches

Chapter Seven: Life Cycle, Reproduction, and FAQs

to perch on, good ventilation and a basking area or two. Check the Care Sheet in the earlier chapters again before you bring home a Panther Chameleon for a pet.

Having a big enclosure does not mean you can add another chameleon in. They don't like company, even if they are from the opposite gender. They will only socialize when it's mating and breeding season, otherwise they will fight each other or stress each other out. To avoid this, don't put them in the same place or put their separate cages near each other.

These are all very basic and you may think that you already know a lot after reading this book, that you won't make the same mistakes. But it happens even to the best people with the best intentions. You cannot say that you know enough—it is always good to be reminded. Taking care of a pet, exotic or domestic, requires that you be cautious and responsible. More importantly, having a pet is not just for your personal enjoyment.

Chapter Seven: Life Cycle, Reproduction, and FAQs

Frequently Asked Questions

How do you calm a hissing chameleon?

You cannot calm a hissing chameleon by patting it on its back or rubbing its tummy. The first thing you should do is to back away from it and respect its space. Then try to understand why the chameleon is hissing so that you can do something about it. It can be because of pain, fear or discomfort.

Why are Panther Chameleons given that name?

They get their names from the markings on their skins that look like those of a panther.

Do Panther Chameleons bite?

Yes, a Panther Chameleon can and will bite when it is scared or threatened. Unwanted or forced handling can be the reason a chameleon will hiss and bite. Significantly, too, this causes stress to the chameleon.

Chapter Seven: Life Cycle, Reproduction, and FAQs

Can Panther Chameleons climb smooth walls?

This is often asked as chameleons are related to lizards. Geckos and anoles can climb level surfaces of walls but chameleons cannot. Their specialized toes are perfect for perching.

Do Panther Chameleons like each other?

Chameleons of the opposite gender can like each other, but those of the same gender rarely do, especially males. They are solitary creatures, not sociable and are best left to themselves. They cannot be kept together in captivity, even if they belong to the same species. Even males and females are housed separately.

Is a chameleon eaten for food?

Generally, chameleons are not human food.

Chapter Seven: Life Cycle, Reproduction, and FAQs

Are Panther Chameleons poisonous?

Panther Chameleons are very unique and they may look weird especially with their 360 degree eyes that can look in two opposing directions individually, but they do not have venom or poison.

Do Panther Chameleons hibernate?

Chameleons do not hibernate as they are native to tropical climates. What they need is appropriate temperatures during the day and night when in captivity so they can get enough rest and sleep.

How fast does a Panther Chameleon move?

A Panther Chameleon is not a fast animal, but its tongue is the world's fastest. It can go from zero to 60 miles in 0.001 seconds, like a sports car or faster.

Chapter Seven: Life Cycle, Reproduction, and FAQs

Are all chameleons from Madagascar?

Not all chameleon species originate from Madagascar but almost half of the known species around the world live there. Some experts believe that all chameleons originated and evolved in Madagascar. Other chameleon species are found in Asia Minor, Mainland Africa and Southern Europe.

Can chameleons regrow their tails?

When geckos, anoles or other lizards get their tails cut either by accident or as means to escape predators, they can regrow them. But the chameleon's long, grasping tail is like a limb that supports the animal's body weight. This appendage, unfortunately, cannot break off on its own then grow back again.

Are chameleon spits sticky?

Yes, a Panther Chameleon's spit is 400 times more glutinous than a human's spit. The chameleon's sticky saliva coats its

Chapter Seven: Life Cycle, Reproduction, and FAQs

whole tongue, helping it to pull and hold on to insects and small animals that it wants to eat.

Do chameleons really walk funny?

Panther Chameleons, like other species have a distinct "jerky walk". They sway their bodies back and forth in an unpredictable, uneven manner. This weird behavior is said to allow the chameleons to imitate the movement of tree leaves and is used as a means to camouflage.

Can chameleons see clearly?

Unlike most reptiles that have poor eyesight and rely on other their senses, chameleons are known to possess a highly developed vision. They can spot objects clearly up to a distance of 10 meters and they also have ultraviolet vision.

Chapter Seven: Life Cycle, Reproduction, and FAQs

Can chameleons live in wintry places in the wild?

You won't find any chameleons naturally living in places where there are extremely cold temperatures. If you would like to study how chameleons live in the wild, you need to go to sub-Saharan African areas.

Are chameleons omnivores or carnivores?

Chameleons love to eat insects, crickets most especially. Panther Chameleons can eve eat up to 40 crickets a day! Some larger species of chameleons have been seen to catch and eat tiny birds and other smaller animals. But you can also see chameleons eating fruit and leaves. Definitely omnivore.

Are chameleons good pets beginners?

If you are looking for your first reptile pet, you should not get a chameleon right away. They have complex needs and are prone to stress. If you are a veteran reptile owner, then it is time to step up your game and get a pet chameleon.

Chapter Seven: Life Cycle, Reproduction, and FAQs

What specie of chameleon should you get for a first pet?

The Panther Chameleon is one of the best choices for a first chameleon pet.

Can all chameleons be kept as pets?

There are more than 180 species of chameleons in the world. Not all of them can be kept as pets. The most common pet chameleons are the Panther Chameleon, Jackson's Chameleons and the Veiled Chameleons. The following species are also kept as pets:

- Carpet Chameleon
- Fischer's Chameleon
- Flap-Necked Chameleon
- Four-Horned Chameleon
- Meller's Chameleon
- Oustalet's Chameleon

Chapter Seven: Life Cycle, Reproduction, and FAQs

What are the basic needs of chameleons in captivity?

First of all, they need a good amount of cage space and regular upkeep. Chameleons in captivity require not just food and supplements but also lighting, humidity control, water source, heating, natural sunlight and basking space.

Conclusion

It is time for a change—add some color into your life by getting a Panther Chameleon for a pet. Owning and taking care of a Panther Chameleon is never easy but it is totally worth it. While they have a reputation of being difficult to maintain, it is not always true. Of course, it is not recommended as a first time pet—but when you get the hang of the requirements, you will find it is the easiest and most satisfying responsibility you could have.

Controlling lighting, heat, humidity, light, water supply, housing, food and nutrients? When you do it daily, and you do it with love, you will find that it is no different compared to caring for other kinds of pets. The only

Chapter Seven: Life Cycle, Reproduction, and FAQs

disparity is that they don't tolerate too much handling and they can be quite delicate when you don't care for them properly. But if you are not too keen on cuddles and you really appreciate a beautiful, exotic creature, you won't regret owning a Panther Chameleon. You only need to plan ahead and plan well—count the cost and be willing to pay the price of raising an exotic pet. When you are diligent in your care, your pet Panther Chameleon will be in good health and live out its life span.

After careful planning, visit a reputable breeder and check out some Panther Chameleons in his care. Who knows, one may capture your eye and your heart—and you may be bringing it home with you!

Chapter Seven: Life Cycle, Reproduction, and FAQs

Photo Credits

Page Photo by user Paul Williams via Flickr.com,

https://www.flickr.com/photos/ironammonite/3996787256/

Page Photo by user Tambako The Jaguar via Flickr.com,

https://www.flickr.com/photos/tambako/8652716285/

Page Photo by user Drea Frei via Flickr.com,

https://www.flickr.com/photos/dreafrei/762491553/

Page Photo by user m.shattock via Flickr.com,

https://www.flickr.com/photos/maryshattock/11566873414/

Page Photo by user Connor Mah via Flickr.com,

https://www.flickr.com/photos/40263796@N05/14788466951/

Page Photo by user Florence Ivy via Flickr.com,

https://www.flickr.com/photos/amalthea23/8960637195/

Page Photo by user vil.sandi via Flickr.com,

https://www.flickr.com/photos/vil_sandi/40153094874/

Page Photo by user Josh More via Flickr.com,

https://www.flickr.com/photos/guppiecat/33123169984/

References

"Panther Chameleon Care Sheet" – ReptilesMagazine.com

http://www.reptilesmagazine.com/Care-Sheets/Lizards/Panther-Chameleon/

"Panther Chameleon" – AnimalSpot.net

http://www.animalspot.net/panther-chameleon.html

"Panther Chameleon" – TheSprucePets.com

https://www.thesprucepets.com/panther-chameleon-1238537"Panther Chameleon" – Durell.org

http://wildlife.durrell.org/animals/reptiles/panther-chameleon/

"How to Set Up Proper Chameleon Enclosure" - muchadoaboutchameleons.com

http://www.muchadoaboutchameleons.com/2012/04/how-to-set-up-proper-chameleon.html

"The Ultimate Panther Chameleon Diet Guide" - Beardeddragontank.com

http://beardeddragontank.com/the-ultimate-panther-chameleon-diet-guide

"Keeping Panther Chameleons" – Exotic – Pets.co.uk

https://www.exotic-pets.co.uk/keeping-panther-chameleons-article.html

"Frequently Asked Questions About Panther Chameleon Care" - Chameleoncaremanual.com

http://www.chameleoncaremanual.com/frequently-asked-questions-about-panther-chameleon-care-guide.php

'Do Chameleons Make Good Pets? What You Need to Know" - Animalbliss.com

https://www.animalbliss.com/chameleons-make-good-pets/

"Breeding Panther Chameleons" - Pantherchameleonworld.com

http://www.pantherchameleonworld.com/breeding/breeding-panther-chameleons/